Baby animals in cities

Bobbie Kalman

Crabtree Publishing Company

www.crabtreebooks.com

Created by Bobbie Kalman

For the skunk kits that swim in our pool,
the squirrel pups that climb our trees, the
raccoon kits that dance on our roof, and the
baby birds that sing along with our music

**Author and
Editor-in-Chief**
Bobbie Kalman

Editor
Kathy Middleton

Proofreader
Crystal Sikkens

Design
Bobbie Kalman
Katherine Berti
Samantha Crabtree
    (front cover)

Photo research
Bobbie Kalman

Print and production coordinator
Katherine Berti

Photographs
Bigstockphoto: p. 4, 24 (foxes)
Tupungato/Shutterstock: p. 20 (left)
M R/Shutterstock: p. 20 (right)
U.S. Fish and Wildlife Service: George Gentry:
    p. 22 (bottom right)
All other images by Shutterstock

Library and Archives Canada Cataloguing in Publication

Kalman, Bobbie
     Baby animals in cities / Bobbie Kalman.

(The habitats of baby animals)
Includes index.
Issued also in electronic formats.
ISBN 978-0-7787-1017-2 (bound).--ISBN 978-0-7787-1029-5 (pbk.)

     1. Urban animals--Infancy--Juvenile literature. 2. Urban ecology
(Biology)--Juvenile literature. I. Title. II. Series: Kalman, Bobbie
The habitats of baby animals.

QL49.K3323 2013   j591.3'92   C2012-908307-0

Library of Congress Cataloging-in-Publication Data

CIP available at Library of Congress

Crabtree Publishing Company
www.crabtreebooks.com   1-800-387-7650

Printed in Canada/012013/MA20121217

Published in Canada
Crabtree Publishing
616 Welland Ave.
St. Catharines, Ontario
L2M 5V6

Published in the United States
Crabtree Publishing
PMB 59051
350 Fifth Avenue, 59th Floor
New York, New York 10118

Published in the United Kingdom
Crabtree Publishing
Maritime House
Basin Road North, Hove
BN41 1WR

Published in Australia
Crabtree Publishing
3 Charles Street
Coburg North
VIC, 3058

What is in this book?

Losing their habitats	4	Not always welcome	16
Baby animals in cities	6	City carnivores	18
Food and water	8	Around the world	20
Where do they live?	10	Helping animals	22
Pets in the city	12	Words to know and Index	24
Feeding wild animals	14		

Losing their habitats

A **habitat** is a place in nature. Plants and animals live in habitats. Many kinds of wild animals have lost their habitats because people have built cities on lands where the animals once lived. Some animals have become **endangered**, which means they are in danger of dying out in the **wild**. The wild is a natural area where people do not live.

Much of the forest where this mother fox and her kits lived has been cut down. This fox family will have to find a new place to live. Will it be in a city?

Moving into cities

Some kinds of animals **adapt**, or adjust, easily to living near humans. Animals that have adapted to living in **urban environments**, or cities, include squirrels, chipmunks, rats and mice, foxes, coyotes, raccoons, skunks, and many kinds of birds. As cities grow bigger and take up more land, animals that are forced out of their natural habitats move into the cities to find food. Living in cities often causes problems for both animals and humans.

Many squirrels and chipmunks find food easily in city parks and people's back yards. Do you have squirrels or chipmunks living near you?

Baby animals in cities

The baby animals on these pages are a few of the animals that live in cities. Some have lost their habitats. Others live in city parks, ponds, back yards, or in people's homes. Which of these baby animals live near you?

chipmunk pup

raccoon kit

skunk kit

opossum joey

squirrel pup

bunnies

red fox
kit

rat pinkies

kitten   puppy

ducklings

Food and water

Animals and their babies need water to **survive**, or stay alive. In most cities, they can find water to drink in ponds, rivers, lakes, puddles, and even in swimming pools. What else do animals need?

These ducklings find plenty of water in a city pond. They also find food to eat in the water and in the park around the pond.

What kind of food?

Animals need food. Some city animals are **herbivores**, or animals that eat mainly plants. Some are **carnivores**, which eat other animals. Animals that eat both plants and other animals are called **omnivores**.

This opossum joey is about to eat some flowers in someone's yard. Opossums also eat insects, worms, eggs, frogs, and dead animals.

Almost any food will do!

Omnivores have the best chance of surviving in cities because they are not fussy eaters. Skunks, squirrels, foxes, raccoons, chipmunks, and opossums are omnivores. Many are also **scavengers**. Scavengers eat any kind of food they find, including dead animals and garbage.

Raccoons find food to eat in garbage cans. They eat almost anything!

Where do they live?

Animals need food and water, but they also need **shelter**. Shelter protects them from bad weather and keeps their babies safe from **predators**. Predators hunt and eat other animals, especially baby animals. Cities have parks and other natural areas where some animals find shelter. Other animals find shelter in people's back yards or even in their homes.

Most cities have trees, and where there are trees, there are squirrels. The mother of these squirrel pups keeps her babies safe in a nest high up in a tree hole.

Skunks often live under people's decks or garages. This skunk family has found shelter in a backyard toy house.

An opossum joey and a raccoon kit meet on the porch of a home. They both live in the same back yard. Will they get along?

Pets in the city

Many city people keep animals as pets. Puppies and kittens are favorite pets. Other pets include hamsters, guinea pigs, mice, rats, bunny rabbits, and parrots. People take care of their pets by feeding them, **grooming**, or cleaning them, and making sure they are healthy.

This young girl is taking her puppy for a walk in the city. She takes good care of her furry friend.

This boy loves his pet kitten, and the kitten loves him, too.

This girl has a bunny for a pet.

*Hamsters are popular pets. They are animals called **rodents**. Rodents have four front teeth that never stop growing. They keep them short with a lot of chewing.*

*This girl rides her pony in the city. The pony lives in a **stable** not far from her house. A stable is a home for horses.*

Feeding wild animals

Wild animals also live near people in cities. Many kinds of birds live in trees, ponds, or on buildings. People enjoy feeding animals such as squirrels, chipmunks, and birds. They especially like feeding baby animals.

This chipmunk pup is being fed seeds. When you feed animals, make sure you remove any wrappers.

Some children have left an apple for a tiny backyard squirrel pup. Squirrels are fun to watch and feed.

This girl is feeding seeds to adult pigeons, but not to their babies.

Fledglings, or baby pigeons, are fed by their parents until they are almost adults. The parents feed the fledglings a liquid they bring up from their throats.

This boy is hanging a bird feeder in front of his apartment building. He will fill it with food for the birds during winter.

15

Not always welcome

Raccoons live in forests and fields, as well as in cities, where they find plenty of food. They make homes for their babies in park or backyard trees and in people's garages or attics. Raccoons can do a lot of damage to homes.

Some people set traps for raccoons and drive them to nearby forests to set them free.

I smell a skunk!

Skunks often live in city parks and neighborhoods. People consider them **pests**, or animals that are annoying. Skunks dig up grass looking for bugs and worms to eat. They also make a bad-smelling liquid in their bodies that they spray when they are afraid. People like to stay far away from skunks!

These skunk kits live under a house with their mother. People try to remove them, but it is very hard.

People do not want mice or rats in their homes. They get into food and can carry diseases. They also have many babies, which then live in the homes, as well. People usually set traps in their homes to kill the mice or catch them in live traps and set them free outside.

City carnivores

Pet dogs and cats are carnivores, but wild carnivores also live in cities. Foxes, coyotes, wolves, and even cougars, have been spotted in most urban areas. What kinds of carnivores have you seen in your city or town?

This cougar is hiding under a car in a parking lot. Cougars can be dangerous to people!

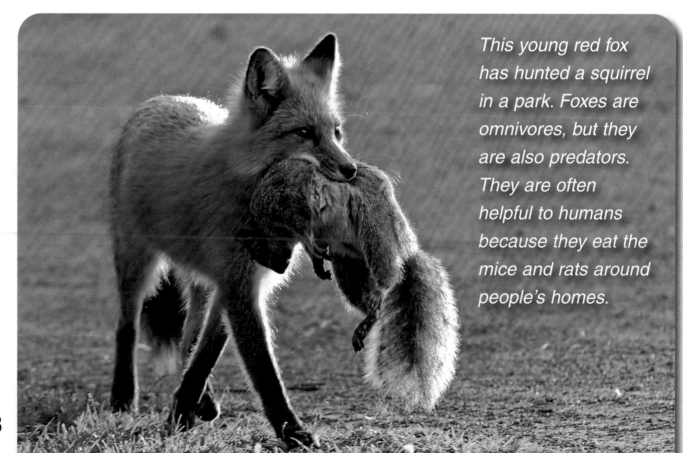

This young red fox has hunted a squirrel in a park. Foxes are omnivores, but they are also predators. They are often helpful to humans because they eat the mice and rats around people's homes.

These coyote pups live in a **den**, or home, underneath a dead log in a city park. They look cute, but they are predators. When they are grown, they will hunt other animals. In many cities, coyotes have killed pet dogs in parks and back yards. Coyotes have also been known to attack humans. It is best to stay away from them!

Around the world

You may see squirrels and chipmunks in your city, but in some cities, you might see deer, cows, monkeys, or polar bears, instead. These animals are treated well by people, who feed them and allow them to wander wherever they wish. In some places, people use them to entertain visitors.

In Nara, Japan, people feed the thousands of sika deer in the city.

*In India, cows are thought to be **holy**, or honored by a religion. They roam freely in cities. Feeding them is believed to bring good luck and wealth.*

Baby monkeys and their mothers can be seen in many cities in India and Thailand. At this old temple, the monkeys are everywhere. Visitors love to feed them.

Some polar bears in the Arctic are starving. They are moving south into cities to find food. This mother and her cubs are looking for food in a garbage dump in Churchill, Manitoba, a city in northern Canada.

21

Helping animals

There are many people who help animals in cities. Some work in zoos, teaching people about endangered animals. Some work in animal shelters that house homeless cats and dogs. Others help wild animals that are injured in cities. Find out how you could help animals in your city.

Many kinds of wild animals live in city zoos. Some zoos have programs for teaching people about endangered animals. Visit a zoo in your city and find out about the programs they offer to help animals.

*Some wildlife groups help endangered animals **breed**, or make babies, so there will be more of them. These red wolf pups were just born.*